The Relentless Pursuit of God in the Midst of Life's Valleys

HOPE CLIMBS

GINA DAVIS

WESTBOW
PRESS®
A DIVISION OF THOMAS NELSON
& ZONDERVAN

WestBow Press books may be ordered through booksellers or by contacting:

WestBow Press
A Division of Thomas Nelson & Zondervan
1663 Liberty Drive
Bloomington, IN 47403
www.westbowpress.com
1 (866) 928-1240

Scripture taken from the New King James Version®. Copyright © 1982 by Thomas Nelson. Used by permission. All rights reserved.

Scripture quotations marked MSG are taken from THE MESSAGE, copyright © 1993, 2002, 2018 by Eugene H. Peterson. Used by permission of NavPress. All rights reserved. Represented by Tyndale House Publishers, a Division of Tyndale House Ministries.

ISBN: 978-1-9736-8332-2 (sc)
ISBN: 978-1-9736-8333-9 (hc)
ISBN: 978-1-9736-8331-5 (e)

Library of Congress Control Number: 2020900333

Print information available on the last page.

WestBow Press rev. date: 01/13/2020

Dedicated to my husband, Richie, my son, Eli, and my daughter, Elisha—I love you always and forever! Also, to everyone who prayed, cried, laughed, and visited us during this hard time.

We will never forget you.

CONTENTS

CHAPTER 1

REACHING FOR HOPE

Rejoice in Hope of the glory of God ... glory in tribulations, knowing that tribulation produces perseverance; and perseverance, character, and character, hope. Now hope does not disappoint.

—Romans 5:2–5 (NKJV)

MY REACH FOR HOPE

It all started on March 6, 2012. I don't like to look back at the calendar because that date and the days to come are filled with images and thoughts I don't want to remember. But for someone who is reading this, I pray you find courage to climb the mountain you may be facing.

I sent my nine-year-old son, Eli, and my seven-year-old daughter, Elisha, to school, just like any other day. They loved going to school, even though it was a new one. We had moved to Cleveland, Tennessee, in October of 2011. My husband, Richie, had just started a new job in Dalton, Georgia, and we were trying to settle into our new home and our new community. The kids had already made a few friends, and we had some great teachers at their new school. As I watched the kids get out of the car that day, I looked at their smiling faces and kissed them goodbye. I had noticed Eli was coughing some, but it seemed like nothing to be alarmed about. He was a very healthy young boy, who was active in basketball, picking on his sister, and tagging along on every activity that I had with the student ministry at our church. A little cough didn't seem like a big deal, but after picking him up from school, I noticed he was not only coughing but also running a fever.

I took him home, put him in bed, and gave him some medicine to reduce the fever. Eli had never been one to complain about taking medicine or getting shots at the doctor's office. He never cried. He had always been very strong and very brave, even as a toddler. I thought to myself, *This is probably just a little bug, and it will go away.*

His symptoms became worse through the night. His fever continued to climb, and the cough was settling deep within his chest. By morning I decided to take him to a mobile health clinic at one of our local schools. I thought he might have the flu or bronchitis. Based on the symptoms he had at that time, a nurse said it looked like bronchitis. The clinic gave us a prescription for antibiotics and said that he could return to school the following week. I remember walking out of that clinic and thinking that something else was wrong. I remember the internal conflict in my mind about whether I was being an overprotective mom or the Holy Spirit was telling me to keep searching. Because I was new to the area, my pastor gave me a recommendation for a local pediatrician. I thought it wouldn't hurt to get a second opinion, so we immediately went to see the new doctor.

As I walked through the doors of the pediatric office, I felt a sense of hope that maybe the doctor could help my son feel better. The doctor stated that he had pneumonia, and he was given stronger medicine. We were also instructed to return if the fever didn't go away during the weekend. Feeling confident that we had a correct diagnosis, we headed home, and the descent into our valley began.

GLORY IN TRIBULATION

In Romans 5:2–3, there are several things that must happen before we can grasp true hope. Verse 3 says that the first thing we have to do is "glory in tribulation." How do we do that? Where is the line between daily trials and a full-blown tribulation? *Merriam-Webster Dictionary* defines trials as "the act of trying, testing, or putting to proof." And it defines tribulation as "a grievous trouble, severe trial, or suffering."

What is the difference? When God has something big to prove to the world, He has to take someone through a big tribulation, to show others that He is the God of the impossible. Without tribulation, we would never know that we can endure hard things. Without tribulation, our character could never grow. Without tribulation, we could never know the hope that doesn't disappoint.

Have you ever been disappointed? I have. Two years prior to this event with Eli, I told our family some very joyful news. I was pregnant with our third child, and even though we were a little surprised, we were very excited to hold this little one in our arms. The pregnancy went well, and I looked forward to the ultrasound that would tell us if we were going to have a little boy or girl. I think my daughter, Elisha, was probably the most excited. She couldn't wait to have a real "baby doll" in the house. She is truly a mother at heart and always trying to help her big brother out. My husband left for a medical mission trip to Peru. We scheduled the ultrasound for our new bundle of joy for a couple days after he would return home. It was important to him to have the whole family at this appointment.

We arrived at the hospital and were all very anxious about getting to see our new baby on the computer screen. The nurse called us to an exam room. Eli and Elisha sat so quietly in the chairs beside me. Richie stood by my head, and we watched with anticipation as the nurse began to measure the baby's bones. My heart was filled with such joy at getting to see our little bundle on the screen, and I loved that my kids were part of this process. The technician began to look for the heart. As she continued to go over the same area multiple times, she said, "I don't see a heartbeat."

What? Surely she was wrong; there had to be one! She kept looking, and my heart felt like it was going to explode. I didn't want to get upset in front of my kids, but I could not hold back the tears. I sat up, and Richie hugged me. The kids saw their mother break down for the first time in their lives. I quickly got up and went to the bathroom. All I wanted to do was hide until this nightmare was over, but we had just entered a dark valley with no mountain in sight.

When I came out of the bathroom, my young children stared at me and wanted answers that I didn't have. Eli looked at me and said, "Mom, maybe she just couldn't find it. Maybe the heartbeat is still there." He wanted to fix this for me, and I wanted to believe that.

Elisha's only words were, "I don't understand, Mom. I don't understand." That was the hardest walk out of any office I had ever faced. Young couples were sitting beside each other, happy and excited, while I wanted to scream. We finally made it to the car. I could hardly breathe. I jumped in the driver's seat and turned on the car. The song that come blaring out of my radio was "Healer." I quickly turned it off and put in a movie for the kids to watch, before trying to find my way out of the parking garage. We didn't make it any farther than just across the road. I had to stop and get out.

My husband, still in a state of disbelief, urged me to call my mentor and friend for support. I will not forget that conversation for as long as I live. I stood outside the car with the phone in my hand, tears running down my face, pain shooting through my heart, and I remember saying, "I still believe. I still believe God can bring this baby's heartbeat back." She agreed with me, and we cried and prayed together.

The next two weeks tested our faith. I spent several days in prayer with people who could agree with me and encourage me. On June 28, we had another ultrasound, but the results were still the same. That day I was admitted to the hospital, and labor was induced. At around 2:00 a.m. on June 29 (my husband's birthday), I gave birth to Ezekiel Davis. The medical report determined that the umbilical cord was wrapped around his neck two times.

I couldn't believe it. The nurse handed me my baby boy, and as I looked over his little lifeless body, he was so perfect, so beautiful. When I held him close, I could still feel the warmth of his little body. I kept thinking, *Just wake up. Wake up!* Even in that moment, I kept saying, "God, You can bring this baby to life!" I watched my husband hold Ezekiel's little body and rock him, just as he had done with our other children. I knew he was praying to God for the same thing.

All we wanted to hear was a baby's cry. We heard them from the other rooms, but our room was silent. The only things to be heard were the sobs and the hopeless cries. There was a sign on our door to let doctors and nurses know that this room had no baby. It was a single teardrop.

As we walked down the halls, the pain was so deep. I wanted to be holding my baby alive and be wheeled out in a wheelchair with him in my arms. But we walked out alone that day. I couldn't even look toward the nursery window as we walked by. I don't recall saying anything to each other on our way home. I just wanted to be with my children, hold them tight, and never let them go.

For many more months I grieved over the loss of our son. The kids tried to be so strong for me. Elisha would get up in my lap, and I would rock her, and she would start to cry. I couldn't even talk to her about it. I couldn't stop my own tears. We would rock and cry, and without saying a word to each other, it was like we both knew what the other was feeling. I couldn't bear being around pregnant women. Well-intended people tried to console me by handing me their babies to hold. Those kind acts were torturous to me because God had taken my baby, and I didn't know why, or even how, to process it.

I remember telling God, "I got You, God! You said that hope will never disappoint. How can that be true if I hoped for my situation to change, and it didn't? I was disappointed, God!"

I heard the Lord speak very clearly to me, saying, "Where was your hope? Was your hope in Me, or was it in your situation changing? When your hope is in Me, I will never fail you, and I will not disappoint you. True hope does not disappoint." The Bible says to put your trust in the Lord—not in test results, not in doctors' reports, not even in your family or friends, but in the Lord God Almighty. If He is almighty, then surely He can take care of me.

I came to understand that I had put my hope and trust not in God but in the outcome of my situation. I had to trust God with everything—even when things didn't turn out like I wanted.

Joseph is a prime example of someone who had to put his trust in God alone. Think about it. He had a dream, his brothers despised him for it, and he was thrown into a deep, dark pit. He must have wondered whether the dream was from God. He had two options: he could believe that God gave him that dream and trust the dream maker, or he could believe that it was just a nightmare because God would never put him in a situation like that. The crazy thing is that was only the beginning of Joseph's problems! God continued to test Joseph, to see whether he really trusted in God or in the pharaoh, the pharaoh's wife, the prison guards, the butler, or his own abilities. At the end of his testing, God used Joseph to save not only his own family but his whole nation.

Why does God test us? What is He testing? What will the test prove?

The Bible has many things to say about God's testing. We see as early as Genesis that there has always been a test for God's people. Look at the tree in the Garden of Eden. Adam and Eve were being tested. Look at the steps of faith Abraham had to make, both into a new country and then eventually up the largest mountain he had ever faced. I imagine the mountain he climbed with Isaac seemed much bigger and harder to climb. I can imagine that with every footstep closer to the top, his feet got heavier and heavier. I don't think he was exempt from Satan's attacks. I believe the same fears that flooded my mind must have flooded his.

There is not anything on this earth more precious than a child. When it's your child that you are carrying to the altar of God, it becomes a lot more personal. We like to think of these stories as cute Bible stories from long ago that don't really apply to us, but I can tell you, we all have an "Isaac" that we must lay down on the altar of God. It may not be a child. It could be a job, a spouse, a relationship, or anything that holds a high position in our hearts. We are asked to lay those things down and believe as Abraham did. Live or die, God will raise him up! Abraham's actions declared that he would obey his God and prove his love by his obedience.

The Bible says obedience is better than sacrifice. Psalm 7:9 in the New King James Bible says, "For a righteous God tests the hearts and minds." Deuteronomy 13:3 says, "For the Lord your God is testing you to know whether you love the Lord your God with all your heart and with all your soul."

What does this say about love and obedience? If we truly love something, then we are more prone to be obedient to it as well. For instance, in a marriage, a wife will be obedient to her husband, not because he rules over her but because she loves him. How does she love him more than she loves having her own way? When he loves her like Christ loved the church, she will do anything for him. That mound of clothes and that pile of dishes won't stand a chance when a wife is truly loved.

This is interesting because Jesus said in Matthew 22:37 that the greatest commandment is to **"love the Lord God with all your heart, with all your soul, and with all your mind"** (NKJV). Is this why Jesus asked Peter the same question three times in the twenty-first chapter of John? Was this a test? Did he answer the question correctly? I believe that many things were happening in that moment on the beach: restoration, healing, and empowering. Most of all, Jesus needed to show Peter that no matter what had happened in the past, Peter's love for Jesus would be his guide.

When we are led by His Love, we will climb the mountain, we will lay our sacrifice down (even with tears and a broken heart), and we will say, "Live or die, I will serve you God." How far, as a church, have we gone from that one truth? With our modern-day conveniences and our padded pews, do we really want to give it up? These are questions that each of us has to face at some point in our lives. In my case, I would face this question over and over again.

THE SLEEPLESS NIGHTS

Our journey toward hope had just begun for Eli. As he was lying in the bed beside me, I reached over with the palm of my hand to check his forehead for a fever. I knew he must have been tired of me touching his face every thirty minutes or so, but a deep concern for my son now flooded my soul. His fever continued to rise through the night, and in addition, new symptoms were arising every hour. Out of nowhere, his little feet and hands began to hurt. I wondered whether he was experiencing growing pains at the same time he had pneumonia. His fever continued to rise, and the pains from his hands and feet where causing him to scream in agony. I had to try something, so I started alternating him from a warm bath for the pain in his joints to a cold bath for the fever spikes. Either way, they both made him cry. All along, he kept begging me not to take him to the doctor. He told me he would be fine if he could just stop hurting and get some rest. However, he could no longer hold down any medication without vomiting. I called the nurse, and she advised us to bring him to the office in the morning.

With no sleep, I loaded Eli and Elisha back into the car for another trip to the doctor. Every time he tried to stand or walk, his muscles would give out and he would fall to the floor. So, like any mother would do, I carried him most of the way.

When we saw Dr. Patty, the pediatrician, we reported the new symptoms. The doctor could see no visible reason for the pain in his hands and feet. She didn't seem very concerned, but I felt desperate at this point. I just wanted the pain to go away, but no one seemed to have an answer. They sent us home again for another very long day with no additional help.

As I continued to care for my son, my thoughts raced about whom to contact, how to pray, and what to do next. All the while, I had a feeling that there was no one who could help, and I felt all alone. If God was trying to develop character in me, how was He going to do it? Every fruit of my spirit was getting squeezed, pushed, and stomped on. The only thing I felt growing now was fear. I was afraid that the doctors were wrong, that I wasn't pushing hard enough for answers, and that I might lose another son if things didn't change.

Our pastors came to visit Eli after the second doctor's visit. He tried to be strong and not show them that he was in pain while they were there. They laid a prayer shawl on Eli and told him to keep it until he got better. One of the pastors wrapped him up in the shawl and prayed that this would soon be over. We believed with them. All the while, I tried to keep my head up. However, I wondered in the back of my mind how I was going to weather this storm. It was not that I thought God didn't hear my prayers, but I have come to realize that if He calmed the every storm for me, how would I ever learn to walk on water?

Eli had another long night with increased pain and fever. Every thirty minutes, his hands would curl up and his feet would hurt so badly that he had to be carried from room to room. This was taking a toll on my emotions. I didn't know what to do but was determined to keep pressing forward. In the morning, I called to see another doctor, and we loaded the car again. This was the fourth doctor we had seen in three days.

The doctor immediately drew blood, gave him a shot, and told us to come back in twenty-four hours. Nothing was helping him, and we had not slept for several days, but I felt better knowing that someone was checking his blood work and trying new medicine.

I was in tears now because I felt that my son was slipping away from me. As I looked into his beautiful, pale, little face, he looked back at me with his big blue eyes and with all the strength in him and he smiled. He kissed my cheek and told me that he loved me; my heart broke. Why couldn't I just fix this? Why couldn't God just fix this? Had He not heard our prayers? Had He not felt my heart? Did He know Eli's pain? Where was God? If He were here, He could make him better!

MARY'S HEART

In John 11, Mary and Martha both said to Jesus, concerning the death of their brother, Lazarus, "Lord, if you had been here, my brother would not have died" (NKJV). Some scholars say this was the same Mary that anointed Jesus with fragrant oil and wiped His feet with her hair in Matthew 26:7. The expense of the oil was a great price for her to pay, but it was no consideration for her as she performed an act of devotion for her Lord. She had given everything to Him! Now, we find her in chapter eleven, and Jesus didn't come when she needed Him most. I felt that I almost understood what Mary might have been thinking.

> *I believed in this man named Jesus! I trusted Him! I gave everything. I physically proved my love for Him! And now, when I need Him the most, where is He? He could have come at any moment while my brother was still alive, and He would have healed him. Why did He not come? Could everything that I thought have been a lie? We asked for Him to come, and we feel like He turned His back on us in our hour of need. I guess He is not the man I thought He was. My brother is now dead, and it has been four days. Will Jesus even come to see us, or is He still too busy? Every day, every hour, every minute that He is not here, my heart is breaking. It is breaking not only for the loss of my brother but for the loss of my hope in something, someone greater. Where are you, Jesus? I*

can no longer stay at this tomb. I will go home where
I can mourn alone. There will be no comfort, and
there will be no peace for me. I trusted in someone,
and now I feel that my trust has been broken. This
pain is too great to bear!

Martha arrives and tells her that Jesus has come. Her thoughts must have raced with excitement, fear, anger. How would she approach Him? How would she say the things that were in her heart? Why would He come now? Was there anything He could do now? She runs to meet him, and the anticipation of the moment almost overtakes her. Her heart beats out of her chest, and the Bible says in verse 32 that she fell down at His feet. This was a place she had been before: first, as an act of love and now as an act of desperation. As she hit the ground, she must have had flashbacks to that moment when she poured out the oil and the tears upon His feet. She must have remembered the reason she would do such a thing. Now the tears fall, but they come from a much different place—a place of hurt, pain, and questioning. How could she ask Him that question? How would He react? She knew in her spirit that Jesus could make it all better, but how? She had to force herself to make the statement that had flooded her soul for four days now. She probably never looked up. She kept her eyes on the feet that had walked on water, the feet that had walked on her heart. She says, "Lord, if you had been here, my brother would not have died." The Bible says that Jesus groaned in His spirit and was troubled. Maybe He thought that out of all the people He touched, she would be the one to believe. How could she ever doubt that He would not come for His friend and come for her? The Bible said that Jesus wept. But out of His weeping came hope, out of His weeping came strength. That strength was not just for Mary, Martha, and Lazarus, but it was also for us today. He understands our fears, He understands our pains, and He most definitely can handle all our questions in a time of need.

FACING YOUR FEAR

I didn't show any fear or concern in front of my family. I couldn't allow them to see how scared I was at that moment. I couldn't allow my daughter, who was watching every move I made, see me lose it!

The next morning, I packed a few things, dropped Elisha off at school, and returned to the doctor's office once again. In the waiting room I looked over at Eli and noticed something was wrong. Eli started complaining about his vision. He told me he was seeing two of everything. I felt fear rising again in my spirit, but I smiled at him and told him everything was going to be okay. I knew deep down that this new symptom was not good.

They took us to an exam room, and he acted so strong for all the nurses and doctors. They asked him how he felt, and his first response was always that he was fine, with the biggest smile he could muster. The doctor was perplexed. His blood work was definitely showing a major problem, but she couldn't pinpoint a diagnosis. She gave Eli another shot and told me, "If this doesn't help, then tomorrow I'm sending him to the hospital." Everything in me wanted to say, "Send him now! I can't handle another night of watching him in pain!"

But our family had started walking in our valley, and like my pastor had always told me, "When you're going through a valley, don't stop; just keep walking." So, I did; I just kept walking—walking with all the fears, all the doubts, with my baby boy in my arms. I just kept walking.

TEST TIME

It's at these moments in time when the Holy Spirit rises up in us and becomes our strength. I hadn't read my bible all week because my test had just turned into a tribulation. If you don't know the answers to the test on test day, then you will probably fail that test. But I was determined that I was not going to fail this test, and I was not going to take this one over. This is why we should study while it is still daytime. In everyone's life, there will come a nighttime or a valley.

The Bible says, **"For we are glad when we are weak and you are strong. And this also we pray, that you may be made complete"** (2 Corinthians 13:9 NKJV). I have to know how to glory and be glad in my weakness because, in that weakness, my God will supply all my needs. In that weakness, He is my El Shaddai. In that weakness, He is my Jehovah Rapha. In that weakness, He is my All in All. He comes on the scene to be my everything. It's in these times that he wants to make us complete. In the *Strong's Concordance,* complete stands for "katartisis," which means improving, equipping, training, disciplining. It includes making the necessary adjustments and repairs.

Obviously God had something in store for my little man's life, for my daughter's life, and for my husband and I because He was needing to complete some things in us. Test time had just started, and my journey toward hope had just begun.

CHAPTER 2

HOPE UNSEEN

For we were saved in this hope, but what is seen is not hope; for why does one still hope for what he sees. But if we hope for what we do not see, we eagerly wait for it with perseverance.

—*Romans 8:24, 25 (NKJV)*

Romans 8 is such a powerful chapter in the bible. Paul speaks about a journey. It was a journey from sorrow to glory. I believe that Paul understood way more than I do about trials, tribulations, and most of all about hope. This is a man who had been blinded, thrown in prison, beaten, shipwrecked, bitten by a snake, and so much more. The man who wrote "I was persuaded that neither death, nor life, nor angels, nor principalities, nor powers, nor things present, nor things to come, nor height, nor depth, nor any other created thing shall be able to separate us from the love of God which is in Christ Jesus our Lord" in Romans 8:38-39 (NKJV) knew something about hope unseen. He did not place his hope in what his visible eyes could see, but instead, he kept his eyes on the prize—the prize that was only found in Jesus.

Was Paul tested? Could he write such words without knowing that every word he just penned was true? I think I could learn something from him when it comes to having hope in something I can't see.

A HOPE FOR ANSWERS

On March 13, 2012, I drove Elisha to school and then took Eli to the doctor's office for the fifth straight day. We packed some clothes for Eli and expected to go to the hospital for a short stay. He kept asking me questions about what it would be like in the hospital. Would they have to give him a lot of shots, what would they do, and was it going to hurt? These were things a normal child would want to know. He felt better after we talked, but I could tell he was still nervous.

I was in such a daze that morning. My husband, Richie, had gone to work, and my pastor called and asked if he needed to come with me. I would have normally said, "No, everything will be fine." But this morning, I agreed, and he met me at the doctor's office.

As we got out of the car, I knew something very bad was happening to Eli, and I knew in my heart that he was going downhill fast. He was now visibly very sick, losing weight, and barely able to walk on his own. He had double vision and an ongoing fever. The doctor told us, "The best place for him now is the hospital. They will figure this out." So, we rushed over to the hospital to be admitted.

It seemed to take forever for the nice lady to put Eli's information into the computer. Eli sat beside me so patiently. I just wanted to get him to a room and with a doctor as soon as possible. Our insurance from my husband's job had just gone into effect on March 1. I didn't even have a card yet. I would realize later that God was watching out for us, even in the small details. They placed a band around Eli's wrist with his name on it and escorted us to his room.

In that small room, we were met by a group of doctors, and after the first round of questions, Eli actually shut his eyes and fell asleep. They put in his IV and started him on fluids. His little body, now down to about fifty-eight pounds, was so exhausted from the pain. His spirit was still so strong though. With every nurse and every doctor, he was so polite, and he would inform them that he was fine and he would be able to go home soon.

With no answers yet from doctors, we began our season of testing (physical testing): blood work, CT Scans, MRIs. I walked Eli through everything the doctors would do. He was so brave. He always had lots of questions, but they answered all of them before anything happened. Eli went to sleep that first night, and I placed my hand on his forehead and kissed it. Wow, no fever! Could this be? It was his first break in fever in days. I had to believe that he was getting better.

As I lay there that night, on the sofa in the hospital room, he woke up just long enough to ask me where I was. He wanted me to get in bed with him, and I happily did. As I snuggled up with him in bed and wrapped my arms around him, being very careful to not disturb all the cords and lines they had put on him, I was taken back to another time when I had felt something very similar.

REMEMBERING HOPE

When Eli was born he was a big baby, weighting nine pounds, eleven ounces. I remember them putting him in my arms and thinking, *He is already a toddler.* But an hour after his arrival, we got some bad news that he was not breathing well and he was in the neonatal intensive care unit. Our hearts sank. This was our first baby, the one God promised us after seven years of infertility. God gave this little one to us. Why was this happening, and where was He? I just wanted to see my baby.

They took us to the NICU, where all the preemies and sick little babies were. When I first took a glance at him, I noticed a clear hood over his head (which was to help him breathe) and all the monitors and cords running from his body. As a new mother, this is not what you want to see. We were told we could not hold him for a while, until they could diagnosis the problem. So I would sit and rub his little fingers. I would look at every part of him. I watched his little chest as it went up and down, taking in the oxygen provided by the hood over his head. I prayed and asked God to touch him and heal him. I wanted so much just to wrap him in my arms and leave that place. I wanted to go home with my baby and start our new lives as a family. I couldn't touch his feet, because of IVs, so I just touched where I could. Richie had to make me leave after hours of sitting and watching. We were given times that we could go back in, and finally, they put him in a new area. This time he was in a little clear box. I looked around at the little preemie babies, and they had plenty of room, but not my Eli. He was already moving, trying to hold his head up, and he was definitely going to grow out of that little box soon.

I remember looking at twins that had been born a couple of days before we arrived. They each weighed two pounds. I saw a picture of the mother inside their box. I would pray for them every time I walked in and always wondered about their story. I never saw any visitors go to see them. What had happened? I was later told that the mother died giving birth. This made me hold Eli even tighter when I got the chance.

For two weeks, the nurses would help me get Eli in and out of that little box, so I could feed him every two hours. The nurses would help situate all the cords around me. I hated those cords, but I remember having such hope that one day soon, we could go home. I would dream about what it would be like for him to lay in his own crib and play with his own toys. I remember leaving the hospital with him after he got better and never wanting to let him go. I know that must have been hard on our family and friends. Everyone wanted to see him, but I had waited for that moment for so long, and I just wanted him all to myself.

I wonder what Mary, the mother of Jesus, thought on that special night when she gave birth to our Savior. Did she truly know how hard it would be, one day, to let him go? I have a feeling she cried like I did, as I sat in a rocking chair, holding my precious son. I was trying not to worry about all the uncertainties of tomorrow and treasure each moment. I was treasuring each smile, each laugh, and each tear. I would hold those things in my heart as well, knowing that we all must grow up. But that day he was my special gift from the Lord.

I think many times we lose sight of those moments in our lives. I can plan for tomorrow, but that doesn't mean I'm supposed to give up on today. My plans may fail, and my circumstances may change, but if I have lived my life for that day, for that moment, then I will have no regrets of what I could have done or should have done yesterday.

So now that baby was nine years old, and I found myself trying to maneuver around cords and hold him once again.

WHERE IS HOPE NOW?

As the morning dawned, I started noticing some things about Eli's body that I had not seen before. He was having trouble using the restroom. I had to hold him in a standing position when he needed to urinate. You could tell he was straining to get anything out. I didn't know at the time, but the muscles in and around his bladder where now being affected by whatever was attacking his body. What was going on? Could it be from just the lack of fluids? I made a mental note, and the nurses came in to take him to have an MRI of his brain.

I picked him up off the bed and put him in the wheelchair the nurse had brought. As we were making our way to the elevator, I looked at him, and I knew something else was wrong. My insides were screaming, *He is not okay!* I looked at his face and noticed that his right eyelid was now opening only halfway. I continued to watch him closely as we made our way to the MRI room. I picked him up again and laid him on a big, flat board connected to the massive machine. They allowed me to stay in the room with him but warned me not to talk to him while the test was being done. They tried to explain that this was going to be a long test, and he would need to lie absolutely still for the next forty-five minutes. Soon, the room was filled with loud bangs and beeps. Hindsight is twenty-twenty, and if I thought I had faced some hard things, this was where my nightmares really started.

HOPE, IN SPITE OF

Romans 8:25 says, **"But if we hope for what we do not see, we eagerly wait for it with perseverance"** (NKJV). I've never been good at waiting, but I was very eager. *Merriam-Webster Dictionary* says perseverance is "a steady persistence in a course of action, a purpose, a state in spite of difficulties, obstacles, or discouragement."

Let's look at one phrase again: "in spite of difficulties." The verse didn't say there would be no difficulties, obstacles, or discouragement. It said in spite of them you will wait eagerly with perseverance. I was definitely trying to stay persistent at one thing—not losing my mind! I had faced some difficulties in my life, but I felt like the situation was more than I could handle.

First Corinthians 10:13 says, **"No temptation has overtaken you except such as is common to man; but God is faithful, who will not allow you to be tempted beyond what you are able, but with the temptation will also make the way of escape, that you may be able to bear it"** (NKJV). Bear it? I must have been confused if I ever thought that being a Christian would keep me from having to deal with life's "hard" things.

Jesus said, **"In this world, you will have tribulation; but be of good cheer, I have overcome the world" (John 16:33 NKJV)**. So, if I live in this world, I will have "hard things" happen, but I can be happy because Jesus has overcome everything in this world. Over two thousand years ago, He died and rose again and took dominion over death, hell, and the grave. Now, all who follow him, no matter what they face in life, will be able to bear it (not with their own strength but God's) and be overcomers in all situations.

The Message Bible says, **"No test or temptation that comes your way is beyond the course of what others have had to face. All you need to remember is that God will never let you down; he'll never let you be pushed past your limit; he'll always be there to help you come through it"** (1 Corinthians 10:13 NKJV).

We need to look at this verse and understand that whatever trials or temptations assault us in this life, if we turn to God in dependence upon Him, He will supply the strength, wisdom, and way to endure them.

CONTINUED DESCENT

Eli was now lying as still as he could. He didn't want to disappoint anyone, but with every minute, the pain in his back grew worse. Over the loud noise of the machine, I could hear him start to cry. My heart was breaking again. If I could just get to him or talk to him, maybe I could ease some fears, but with each movement, the test would have to stop. This was not a normal cry. This was a cry of pain and I knew he was really hurting. I started to pray, and only God could understand this prayer. I had no words that could help him, but the Holy Spirit could pray exactly what was needed in the moment.

His cries got louder and louder. Over a speaker, the technician kept telling him he only had to lay there another five minutes and the test would be over. But his back was hurting so badly at this point that he couldn't lay still. She stopped the test and came in to talk to him, but when she saw my face and the tears running down, she knew that we were both done.

In those moments I had prayed every prayer that I could pray, and now it was my moans and groans that the Holy Spirit would have to help me with. Romans 8:26 says, **"Likewise the Spirit also helps in our weaknesses. For we do not know what we should pray for as we ought, but the Spirit Himself makes intercession for us with groanings which cannot be uttered"** (NKJV).

When they got Eli back into the wheelchair, I felt an urgency to get him to his room and find the doctors. What was only minutes seemed like forever as I watched Eli start to slur his words. Half of his mouth was not moving now, and his eyes were not tracking together anymore. The inside of me was screaming, *I have to find a doctor now!* We wheeled him back up to his room, which was filled with grandparents, my husband, and our pastor. They put him in bed, and I rushed to find the nurse. I pulled her outside the room so Eli wouldn't see the panic on my face, and she knew something was wrong. She ran into the room, took one look at him, and pushed the red button. All the doctors came running.

Right then, I knew my job as mom, the one who can fix everything, was over. I couldn't fix this. I didn't know how to stop it, and all I felt was the urgency for someone to figure this all out and stop this process. I didn't know it at the time, but I was seeing his body shut down from the inside out.

They took me, my husband, and our pastor into a room, and the doctor said, "We think we know what this is. It's called Guillain-Barré syndrome, and your son's body is attacking itself from the inside. The bad cells are starting to eat away at every nerve ending in your son's body, and soon he will be totally paralyzed. The good news is that it should all come back, but it may be a very slow and long recovery time. You may be looking at a year before everything returns." I know I didn't hear everything the doctor said because I was thinking that I didn't care how long it would take, I just wanted them to save his life now. I knew that this wasn't the worst to come, but I wanted him in that ICU unit stat!

I don't think I had ever wanted something so badly, so quickly. I wanted God to fix everything now! There was no time to spare! If something didn't happen soon, I would be looking at putting another son in a grave with a tombstone that could only say one thing: "Why?"

I knew Eli was secure in the Lord. He gave his heart to Jesus when he was five years old. His daddy was in Africa, building churches at the base of Mount Kilimanjaro, and when he returned home, Eli couldn't wait to tell him what Jesus did in his heart. He was filled with the Holy Spirit when he was six years old at the Ramp in Hamilton, Alabama. He had prayed for me and others on numerous occasions, and the Lord had answered his prayers. Where was my "God of Hope" now? I couldn't see Him, and I couldn't feel Him. I asked that He would give the doctors guidance as they took care of my baby boy.

In Matthew 8:23–27, the disciples of Jesus find themselves on a boat in the middle of what the Bible calls a "great" storm (NKJV). Their master, leader, mentor, and friend were on the boat fast asleep. The boat was being covered with waves, and the disciples came to Jesus saying, "Lord, save us! We are going to die!"

Still lying there, he looked at them and said, "Why are you fearful, O you of little faith?" Jesus got up and rebuked the winds and the sea, and the Bible said there came a great calm.

First, when we are going through storms, we have to realize that if we have asked Jesus to come into our hearts and be our Lord and Savior, then He is always on our boat. He said He would never leave us or forsake us, especially in the middle of life's storms. Some of these disciples were fishermen by trade. I'm sure they had been through some storms in the sea before, but the Bible said this was a great storm, and even the most experienced of fishermen that night were scared for their lives.

Even the strongest Christians today can be rocked by the storms that arise in their lives. No one is exempt from the storms. In the parable, found in Matthew 7, Jesus taught about a man who built his house on the rock and another man who built his house on the sand. They both got hit by the same storm, but only one made it through. Why? The wise man built his house on the rock, and it was steady on its firm foundation.

Sometimes God calms the storms, but sometimes He calms us. It's easy to say we have faith and we believe when we are not facing a great storm, but it's only when we are tested in the storms of life that we truly know what we believe. We are all human, just like the disciples, and we can't get too comfortable when the waters are smooth.

The Bible said there came a "great calm" (Matthew 8:26 NKJV). We can only have a great calm when we have had a great storm. Jesus is the Great Calm. There was another storm in Matthew chapter 14, but this time Jesus didn't rebuke the storm. He simply said, "Come." He wants us to keep our eyes on Him, and He will show us that He can bring us through even the worst storms. Sometimes He says "Calm," and sometimes He says "Come." God wants us to be water walkers. If He calmed every storm we faced, we would never know how to walk on the water through them. So, He calms us and tells us to "come." Even if we start to sink, He reaches out His hand and saves us.

GREAT CALM

I needed one of those great calms at this moment! I didn't want to walk through this one, but we don't get to choose the storms or the mountains that we face. God just says we have to know how to walk through them and move them.

Eli wrote a speech once on being brave. One of the lines he quoted from Ambrose Redmoon was, "Courage is not the absence of fear, but rather the judgment that something else is more important than fear." Eli continued by saying, "It's doing what you are afraid to do. It's having the power to let go of the unfamiliar and forge ahead into new territory." Right now, I had to have the courage to keep moving, keep believing, keep breathing.

The nurses from the pediatric intensive care unit came down and put his little body on a bed. He begged me to stay right by his side. I promised I would not leave him, and I grabbed his hand. He held onto mine as tightly as he could, just to make sure.

We entered into the PICU room, and he started to get nervous. There were a lot of people moving and doing things, and no one was telling him anything because they didn't have time. He was going down fast, and we had just entered into the darkest place in the valley.

I was having a hard time seeing any light from here. I was having a hard time seeing hope anywhere. God never promised we would always see: **"Though I walk through the valley of the shadow of death, I will fear no evil, for You are with me" (Psalm 23:4 NKJV).** The Bible also says, "If I say, my foot slips, Your mercy, O Lord, will hold me up. In the multitude of my anxieties within me, Your comfort gave me renewed hope and cheer" (Psalm 94:18–19 NKJV).

I needed some renewed hope because the next thing I experienced gave me nightmares for months after it occurred. They performed on Eli what is called a "niff" test. I cannot even type what I saw in my little boy's eyes when they did that. The test gives a reading of his lung capacity. Can you imagine seeing your child suffocated ... on purpose? Not just once, but this test was done three times to check for accuracy. I cannot explain to you what I was going through when I looked at his face during this test, with him begging me, "Mom! Please don't let them do that again to me!" My heart hurt for him, knowing they had to do it. Dear God! Where are you? Please! Come to his rescue!

His lungs were getting weaker by the second. At this point I had not cried or shown any fear in front of Eli. I needed to be strong so that he could be strong. The primary physician pulled my husband out first and talked with him. I was next but not ready to hear what he had to say. Eli kept asking if I would come back, and I assured him I would return in just a minute.

The doctor proceeded to tell me that Eli's body was shutting down. He said they could not stop this process, and if they didn't go ahead and induce a comma and put a tube in his lungs, he would die on the table. He felt the time was short, and we needed to say our goodbyes just in case he never awakened.

OUT OF OUR HANDS

I couldn't believe that this was happening! Just a week before, we were laughing and playing, and Eli was healthy. Now he was dying right before our eyes. And neither my husband nor myself or the doctors could stop this process—only God.

CHAPTER 3

ANGELS OF HOPE

Be of good courage, and He shall strengthen your heart, all you who hope in the Lord.

—Psalm 31:24 (NKJV)

I took a deep breath, and I walked back in the room, where my husband was talking to Eli. I heard him say, "Eli, they are going to give you some medicine, and it's going to make you sleepy. While your body is resting, trying to get better, I want you to fight. Don't give up, son! Don't quit! We love you, and Jesus is with you. Your mom and I will be right here with you."

With all the nurses standing very intently around us, Eli looked at me, and I had a little tear running down my cheek. He said with a sweet voice, "Mom, I just want to go home. I'm okay. Can you just take me home now? Please?"

Oh, how I wanted to grab him, take him in my arms, and walk out with everything okay, but he was in God's hands now. He was always in God's hands. God just let us borrow him for a little while, to raise, mold, and train up in the way he would go. But most of all, it was to show him God's love, to love him the way God loves us. I wasn't feeling like God loved me at that moment. I didn't want it to end there.

I kissed his little face, and I made him a promise that, when he woke up, I would take him home. I didn't know at the time how hard that promise would be to fulfill.

It was one thing to for me to try and fulfill a promise, but it was another thing when God promised. The Bible says that God is faithful, that His compassions fail not. They are new every morning and great is His faithfulness. The Lord is our portion, and our hope is in Him.

Deuteronomy 7:9 says, "Therefore, know that the Lord your God, He is God, the faithful God who keeps covenant and mercy for a thousand generations with those who love him and keep His commandments" (NKJV).

I am reminded of an old hymn:
"Great is Thy faithfulness,"

O God my Father,
There is no shadow of turning with Thee;
Thou changest not, Thy compassions, they fail not
As Thou hast been, Thou forever wilt be.

Summer and winter, and springtime and harvest,
Sun, moon and stars in their courses above,
Join with all nature in manifold witness
To Thy great faithfulness, mercy and love.

Pardon for sin and a peace that endureth,
Thy own dear presence to cheer and to guide;
Strength for today and bright hope for tomorrow,
Blessings all mine, with ten thousand beside!
"Great is Thy faithfulness!"
"Great is Thy faithfulness!"
Morning by morning new mercies I see;
All I have needed Thy hand hath provided—
"Great is Thy faithfulness!"
"Lord, unto me!"[11]

At that moment, I needed God to be faithful to the words that had already been spoken over Eli and over our family. So, I did as Hebrews 10:23 says to do: **"Let us hold fast the confession of our hope without wavering, for He who promised is faithful"** (NKJV).

---

[1] Ren. *Faithfulness*. Carol Stream, IL: Hope Publishing Co., 1923.

KEEP CLIMBING

I held Eli's hand and told him I loved him as they gave him the medicine that would put him to sleep. As soon as his eyes closed, they rushed my husband and me out of the room. For the first time in days, I broke down. Richie held me tightly, and neither of us could utter a word. We just cried. What was happening? Why our son? We had just obeyed God months before to pick up everything and move to Cleveland, Tennessee. For the past ten years, we had done mission work all over the world. Somewhere in my mind I thought that working for the Lord would keep me from troubles. That thought is not based on scriptures. John 16:33 says, **"In the world you will have tribulation; but be of good cheer, I have overcome the world"** **(NKJV)**. Jesus told us that if we follow Him we will have troubles. The good news is that even in those troubled times, we can be happy knowing that Jesus has overcome all of our troubles!

The nurse took us back down to Eli's old room until we could go see him again. I sat on his bed as Richie went to make some phone calls and talk with our family. I sat there in such numbness, not knowing what to do or say. I was the strong one. I was the one that tried to keep everything and everyone together, and until this moment, I had never felt so weak.

The door opened, and in walked our pastor with her arms open wide. She held me tightly as I wept uncontrollably. All the fears from losing my baby boy two years before came to the surface, and I remember telling my pastor, "I don't want God to take Eli—not now!" She held me until the doctors said it was time to see him.

They took us to see Eli, and we entered into his room, where he was hooked up to many different machines. But something was different when we walked in. It was like we stepped into something I had never felt so strongly before. I entered into the tangible peace of God that surpasses all understanding. It was a peace I had never felt before, and it made me hopeful. Somehow, looking at him lying there, resting, even if it was with a machine, gave me peace. It was unspeakable peace that surrounded him and surrounded us as we kissed him and touched him and told him we were there.

These are the moments when we must not look at what is seen but what is unseen. The Bible says, "While we do not look at the things which are seen, but at the things which are not seen. For the things which are seen are temporary, but the things which are not seen are eternal" (2 Corinthians 4:18 NKJV).

I was constantly reminded to look deep within my spirit and speak out into that room what I did not yet see. So what did I see when I looked deeply? I saw Eli, and he was running and playing on a beach, and he was well and whole again. I could not get used to the tubes because he was going to come out and come through this.

We take so many things for granted with our kids. I just wanted to see his big blue eyes open up and look at me again. I wanted to see that smile return to his face again, and I wanted to hear his voice again, no matter what he was saying. At this point, I would have taken a squeeze of the hand or a nod of the head, but we had nothing except a hope that was deep down in our hearts and peace that surpasses all understanding. This hope that I was searching for was not something I could put my physical hands on, but it was a hope that I found in the midst of His amazing peace and amazing grace that filled the room.

GOD SENDS HIS ANGELS

Angels are mentioned all throughout the Bible. If anyone ever needed one, Eli sure needed one now. Angels were created for many things; some were created for worship and praise, like we see in Isaiah 6:1–3 (NKJV). When Isaiah saw the Lord sitting on His throne, he also saw seraphim above it, and each one had six wings. Two of their wings covered their faces, two more covered their feet, and the other two were used to fly. They would cry aloud, saying, "Holy, holy, holy is the Lord of hosts; the whole earth is full of His glory!" They were worshiping God and giving Him praise! Revelation 4:8 goes on to say that there are angels who do not rest day or night, but they continually say, "Holy, holy, holy, Lord God Almighty, Who was and is and is to come!" (NKJV).

Some angels were sent to guide us. If we look at Matthew, chapters 1 and 2, you will see that angels gave instructions to Joseph about the birth of Jesus. Philip was given instructions by an angel in Acts 8:26, and Cornelius was also instructed in Acts 10:1–8 (NKJV).

Other angels came to meet physical needs. God sent angels to minister to Jesus in Matthew 4:11: **"Then the devil left Him, and behold, angels came and ministered to Him" (NKJV).**

The *Spirit-Filled Life Bible* says, "There are more direct references to angels in the New Testament than in the Old Testament. Jesus talked about angels (Matthew 26:53, Mark 13:32, Luke 20:34–36, and John 1:51 NKJV) and not only were angels in attendance at His birth, resurrection, and ascension, they were active amid the early church's life. In Acts, angelic activity freed those imprisoned for their faith, led Philip to an evangelistic opportunity, told Cornelius how to find

Peter in order to hear the gospel, struck judgment on wicked Herod, and encouraged Paul during a killer storm. Throughout the New Testament, believers are given instruction on the presence, nature, and function of angels, fallen and unfallen."

But right now, Eli needed an angel of protection. He needed the angel who showed up in the fire with Shadrach, Meshach, and Abednego in Daniel 3. He needed the angels who showed up as Daniel was thrown into the pit of lions in Daniel 6. Eli's life hung in the balance, and with our natural eyes, we were going to lose him.

ANGEL OF PROTECTION

It had now been one week since Eli first showed signs of fever and a cough. How did we go from perfectly healthy to an intensive care unit, on a ventilator, struggling to even stay alive, in seven days? With little to no sleep, it was only by God's power that I was able to function.

The first night in the ICU was hard. They allowed me to stay on a foldout chair that was placed in the corner of the room. It was a fairly large room with a long counter behind the bed, which ran the whole length of the room. Lots of machines were placed around the bed. On the other side of the room were glass doors with glass windows everywhere. They all had blinds on them, but most of the time the doors stayed open so the nurses could monitor Eli. Next to his room was another smaller room that was only illuminated at night.

Eli had feeding tubes, a catheter, heart monitors, two IVs, and a ventilator. He was not moving at all. They had given him enough medicine to keep him sedated until they could get a definite diagnosis and see if his body would start to respond to any treatments.

On the rails of the bed, there where straps that they would put around his wrists to hold his hands down, just in case he woke up and tried to pull out any of the tubing. So here he was, lying on this bed, only wearing some hospital pants. If he were to awake, he would not be happy about those "hospital pants." That's what they call diapers to big boys who would never be caught wearing such things. He was such a modest little boy. He never liked running around without a shirt, and even as a toddler, you would never catch him running around naked in our house. I couldn't wait to get a hospital gown on him, just in case he woke up. They were not going to allow anything on him so soon, but my heart just wanted to take care of him and hold him again.

Every time the nurse came in, I watched everything she did. I would get up and stand beside Eli and rub his hands and his feet. I would continue stretching them, just as we had done before, but this time I would not hear him say, "That feels good, Mommy," or "Thank you, Mommy. I love you." Oh, how I missed his voice. I missed looking into those blue eyes and hearing his contagious laugh. He would often tell jokes, just to make himself laugh. There was no laughing now, only beeping noises and the sound of the machine that was now breathing for him.

I soon learned how to rotate Eli's body every hour, so he wouldn't get bedsores. I also learned how to change his sheets and give him a bath with all the tubes attached. The nurses would have loved working with Eli if he were awake. They knew I was taking good care of him. The only things that weren't affected in Eli's body were his heart and his mind. Every other part of his body was paralyzed or shut down.

WHERE ARE YOU?

In Psalm 10:1, the psalmist asked the same question that I asked myself over and over again: **"Why do you stand afar off, O Lord? Why do you hide in times of trouble?" (NKJV)**. The Message Bible says, "God, are You avoiding me? Where are You when I need You?" How many times do we think we are alone in our struggle to understand where God is when we can't see Him? The Bible shows me every day that I'm not the only one who asked the hard questions, and faces insurmountable odds. I'm not the only one who has asked God why. If you read on to Psalm 11:1, it says, "In the Lord I put my trust" (NKJV). In all my doubts, I trust the Lord. In all my fears, I trust the Lord. In all my failures as a wife and a mother, I trust the Lord. So at that moment, I put all my trust in the Lord to take care of Eli, to take care of Elisha, and to take care of me.

POSITIVE DIAGNOSIS

The doctors were still perplexed at the symptoms that Eli had. They immediately did a spinal tap to help them verify that this was in fact Guillain-Barré. We didn't have the test results for several hours, so any treatment was postponed until the test results were received. Several doctors that were working on him had come from Children's Hospital in both Boston and Chicago. The statistics say only one in one hundred thousand children Eli's age come down with this syndrome. They had seen a few cases before but offered us little hope of "full" recovery. Many children cannot even walk after a year, and some have relapses and the process starts again. I'm glad I didn't know that then. My only concerns were making sure he was comfortable and waiting for him to show some signs of life.

It says in Isaiah 40:29, God "gives power to the weak, and to those who have no might, He increases their strength" (NKJV). Verse 31 goes on to say, **"But those who wait on the Lord shall renew their strength; they shall mount up with wings like eagles, they shall run and not be weary, they shall walk and not faint."** I was holding on to this scripture and holding onto the promise that He would give Eli His strength because Eli himself had none. I was holding onto that promise for me as well.

The news came back that the first spinal tap was clear. They were expecting to see elevated protein levels, which would confirm the Guillain-Barré diagnosis. What now? They started working overtime, reading articles in the medical journals, telling us that Eli would need another spinal tap in a couple of days, to get an updated result. But until then, we had two choices. Eli could have a full blood transfusion, which would be an eight-day process; he would have to remain on the ventilator and in a coma state for that period of time. Or we could do what they called an IVIG treatment; this procedure would only take two days, depending on Eli's response to the treatment.

I remember walking in and out of the ICU waiting area, where we frequently had lots of visitors, which included grandparents, pastors, and friends. Everyone understood that I was not going to leave Eli's side, except for short moments to go to the restroom. I was so thankful for all the visitors, but my only thoughts were on that little boy lying in that bed.

We informed those who were waiting to please pray with us that the doctors would know for sure what this was and start a treatment on him soon. Within hours of that prayer, the doctors found documentation that some similar cases had existed, and we could proceed with the IVIG treatment. The diagnosis changed. It became Guillain-Barré with a Miller Fisher variant. The Guillain-Barré was attacking his body from his feet up, and the Miller Fisher was attacking his eyes, facial muscles, and ability to swallow. So Satan was working overtime to take Eli out from both directions. Later, after doing some more research, I discovered that only one in five million children Eli's age would ever get this exact diagnosis.

With a treatment plan in place, I tried to lie down on the foldout chair in the corner. With every beep of the machines, I would ask God to help him. I was trying not to look at all the numbers on every monitor, but I knew the important ones. So, my eyes stayed glued to his respiration rates and his heartbeat. When I had a second to think, all I could do was cry. I couldn't read; I didn't want to talk; I couldn't even pray. There is a point in our valleys when God understands our hearts. He hears our cries and understands the pain we are feeling and the sheer disbelief of what is happening. Fears entered into my mind, and I couldn't even fight them. I had never felt so helpless, so hopeless, so scared. What if … what if God took my little Eli home? How would I make it? How would I explain this to Elisha? Elisha and I both had a very hard time just two years earlier, when we lost her baby brother, Ezekiel. I had thought I was over it, but this situation pulled out every insecurity I had ever had.

ENCOUNTER

At 2:00 a.m., I was lying with my eyes wide open, waiting for the nurse to come in and turn his little body again. All of a sudden, I heard something fall to the floor from behind his bed. I sat up and looked around. No one was in the room but me and Eli, so I asked God, "What was that?" Immediately, it was like a veil was lifted from my eyes, and behind his bed stood the most amazing, strong, and powerful angel. He was as tall as the ceiling, and when he leaned over Eli's head, his wings extended out. As he extended, his wings brushed along the counter and pushed a pen onto the floor. We were in the largest room in the intensive care unit, and the angel's wingspan went the full length of the room. He stood in power, with his full uniform on. Hanging on his left side was a quiver that held his huge silver sword. As he leaned over intently, as to prepare for battle, he reached his right arm down across his body and pulled out his sword. He brought it up to his right ear, as if preparing to swing, while leaning over my son's lifeless body. I then glanced up and saw something that I cannot explain. It was as if darkness itself was trying to enter Eli's room from above. This darkness was coming in every corner, and it was coming closer to my son. But just as quickly as the darkness was trying to come in, the angel of the Lord took one swipe across Eli's body and the darkness left the room. The angel then took his sword and continued to stand ready for anything else that might try and come into that room.

I couldn't believe what I was seeing! Was this for real? Was I dreaming? No, I was wide awake! So I asked God, "Who is this?"

The Lord replied, "This is the angel of protection that the saints of God have prayed for. Nothing else will come against your child."

A peace entered my heart and entered that room. At that moment, I knew Eli was going to wake up, and no matter how long it took for him to get better, he was not going to die. So for the first time in days, I was able to shut my eyes for a short rest.

CONFIRMATION

At 5:00 a.m., I received a text from a close friend. She said that all night a word had stirred inside her for me, and she waited until then to share it. The word was, "God will not fail you." Again, it seemed God was continuing to confirm to me that he was with me and he would not fail me. All my fears were now gone. I was just waiting in expectation for when I would see Eli's eyes again, when I would hear his voice, and when I could feel him squeeze my hand again. I didn't care at this point how long it would take. I was ready to see Eli show some signs of life again.

UPWARD JOURNEY

It seemed that in the Spirit realm, everything had changed, even though in the natural, nothing had changed. I felt our ascent upward was just now starting, and this was going to be a big mountain to climb. With my heart full of joy and my mind full of peace, I knew that whatever we had to face now, God was with us, and He was going to lead us home!

CHAPTER 4

HOPE ENDURES

Therefore we also, since we are surrounded by so great a cloud of witnesses, let us lay aside every weight, and the sin which so easily ensnares us, and let us run with endurance the race that is set before us, looking unto Jesus, the author and finisher of our faith, who for the joy that was set before Him endured the cross, despising the shame, and has sat down at the right hand of the throne of God.

—Hebrews 12:1 NKJV

HOW DO I ENDURE THE VALLEY?

I believe God is looking for people who will endure the hard things, seek the glorious things, and give the precious things. To be honest, I had endured some hard things, and I loved seeking the glorious things, but I didn't want to even think about giving the precious things—not when it came to my children. "I'll give you money, but don't mess with my kids, God." I had a lot to learn and the Heavenly School House was just now starting. My teachers name was Holy Spirit.

So, what is endurance? If I must run this race, then it might help me to understand how to "run with endurance." At that moment, I just wanted to pick up my son and run—run away from the hospital and run away from all the problems. *Merriam-Webster Dictionary* defines endurance as "the ability to last, the ability to withstand pain, distress, fatigue, and hardship."

Hebrews 10:35–36 says, **"Therefore do not cast away your confidence, which has great reward. For you have need of endurance, so that after you have done the will of God, you may receive the promise" (NKJV).** So, as I see it, on one mountain I have "doing the will of God," and on the other mountain, I have "receiving the promise." We need endurance for the gap. Now, please don't get me wrong. I don't believe in a "works" type of gospel. Everything I have ever received from God was because of His grace. I understand that bad things happen to good people because we live in a fallen world. It's still His grace that wakes me up in the morning, and it's His grace that helps me do His will. It was His grace that saved a wretch like me. But with that being said, we need endurance so we will be able to behold "the Promise."

I don't believe God would ever ask us to do anything that He Himself had not done before. Let's examine that thought. Psalm 9:7 says, "The Lord shall endure forever," so He Himself endures (NKJV). Psalm 72:17 says, "His name shall endure forever," so His Name endures (NKJV). Psalm 100:5 says, "For the God is good. His mercy is everlasting and His truth endures to all generations," so His truth will even endure (NKJV). Isaiah 40:8 says, "The grass withers, the flower fades, but the word of our God stands forever," so His very word stands or endures forever (NKJV).

So if God Himself, His name, His truth, and His word endure forever, then do you think we might be able to endure some hard things just for a little while? "For I consider that the sufferings of this present time are not worthy to be compared with the glory which shall be revealed in us" (Romans 8:18 NKJV). Paul wrote that knowing that Jesus Himself endured everything. Everything you and I face today, Jesus already paid the price for it. Heartache, pain, abandonment, loneliness, and sickness were thrust on His body at the cross. That's why when we go through things, we can be sure that we are not alone. Jesus didn't promise that we wouldn't face storms, but He did promise He would not leave us or forsake us! That's the good news!

NEXT STEP

My every waking moment was now spent watching my son's lifeless body on that ICU bed. Would the treatments work? We continued to pray that he would show some great improvements.

In the *Spirit-Filled Life Bible,* Jack Hayford points out that as we walk in faith, we must learn to see our present circumstances in light of the future promises of God. Though we are works in progress now, we have hope knowing that God will complete the work He is doing in us. We can endure suffering now because we know that it is momentary compared with the eternity we will spend in the glorious presence of Jesus. We can be content in every circumstance now, knowing that we will have all of God's riches in glory. We walk by faith and set our eyes on Jesus until we see Him face to face.

Philippians 1:21 says, **"For to me, to live is Christ, and to die is gain" (NKJV).** We should not fear death because being in heaven with Jesus will be wonderful. We should seek to live each day on earth for the purposes and glory of Jesus Christ. What can I do today to give glory to God? How can I prove to a lost and dying world that God is who He says He is and He will do what He said He would do?

I had to keep my eyes on the prize. What did that look like when I looked at Eli? What did I see in the spirit when I closed my eyes? When I closed my eyes and laid the current situation down in front of Jesus, I could look beyond my present situation, and I could see what God wanted me to see. I saw a white sandy beach. On the beach, I could see my whole family playing together. Off in the distance, I could see someone running toward me with his arms open wide. The closer he gets, I recognize that it's my son! He has no limp, no problems running, jumping, or swimming. His feet and body are perfectly normal. I just sit with my husband, and I watch Eli and Elisha play together. Oh, what a day that will be! However, my eyes opened, and I saw what I was facing. In the natural, I feel it is impossible, but my spirit screamed, **"All things are possible to him that believe" (Mark 9:23 NKJV)**. So I took a deep breath, and I pulled up my chin and faced another day. I watched and waited to see what God was going to do in that moment.

Would all of Eli's body recover at once, or would it just be one thing at a time? Even Ezekiel stood in a valley of dry bones, and I bet he wondered the same thing: How are you going to do this God? And it wasn't until he watched bone connect to bone, muscle to muscle, and then flesh to flesh that it all happened. God could have just made those men appear out of nowhere, but what was He trying to show Ezekiel? There were many lessons to learn from this story. One might have been that when God tells you to prophesy over something, it will come to pass—maybe not how you expected, but it will happen. God will bring it to pass! I didn't know how God was going to do it, but I knew I was going to have to endure this process until I saw with my natural eyes what my spiritual eyes had seen.

So, I prophesied! We kept calling Eli back. I would turn the speakerphone on with my friends, and they would pray into that hospital room. I laid my iPad right by his head and played a song that continued to remind me and Eli that it was not over until God said it was over.

THE SOUND OF HOPE

Just a couple months prior to Eli's sickness, our family was able to meet Ricardo Sanchez. I didn't know he had written a song about his own son's journey back from sickness, entitled "It's Not Over." We got to meet Ricardo before a worship service, and Eli was able to talk with him. Eli had been playing the guitar for about a year, and he loved to watch Ricardo play. We took their picture together, but in my wildest dreams, I could have never imagined that our paths would meet again. But this time, it was in a cold intensive care unit room, on my son's pillow.

The music echoed through the sounds of the ventilator and the beeps coming from all the machines. It bounced off the glass windows and back to my ear as my head was lying gently on Eli's chest. I just kept singing it and playing it, until my heart believed it. We had placed pictures of Eli in the room as a reminder of what he looked like before his eyes didn't track together, before his face drooped on one side, and before he couldn't speak or walk. Two days passed, and it was time for another spinal tap and a series of MRIs.

ENDURING FEAR

I'll never forget when they were getting ready to take Eli for his first MRI since being on a ventilator. They told me they would have to lower his dose of medicine that was keeping him asleep, and someone would manually breathe for him, using a bag, while they got him to the MRI machine. They also said they would put him fully under again for the test, and someone would sit and give him air for two hours, while this test was going on. Now I trust God, but I wasn't so sure if I trusted someone else sitting there pumping air into my son's lungs. What if they got tired? What if they stopped? I didn't feel comfortable with this at all, but I had no choice but to trust them and trust God. I guess you could say that I may be a little controlling when it comes to my kids. I would have happily taken a crash course on pushing air into that little bag that helped my son stay alive, but they didn't offer that to me.

They informed me that when he came off his medicine, he might try to move. The medicine was lowered, and the bag was placed on his ventilator tube. Leaving him in his bed, we took off down the hall, into the elevators, and down many hallways. With every bump, I watched my baby's body move, and I couldn't wait to get this over with. We reached the room where the team of anesthesiologists was ready to do their job. The nurses called me over to sign some papers, and while I was standing at the counter, a lady came running up to me and said, "We need you now!" What was wrong? I couldn't move fast enough to get to him. I entered the room, and his head was moving side to side. His eyes were not open, but the nurse told me to talk to him. I placed my hand on his hand, and I leaned down really close to his face and said, "Hey, Eli, this is mom. I'm right here with you. I love you!" He immediately recognized my voice and started calming down. I watched a tear come down the side of his face, and I gently wiped it away. Now I had tears coming down onto the sheets of his bed, but I made sure my voice was calm. Wow! He had heard my voice, and he was there! The doctors then put him under general anesthesia, and his little body was still once again.

They ushered me out into the waiting area, where I would be for two and a half hours. I called a friend, who is also a pastor, to help me press through during this time. You have to realize, Eli had not left my side, even for a second, over the last nine days. I felt a flood of emotions. I felt sad, scared, and lonely. I continued to question God as to why we had to go through this. I remember feeling better after talking and praying with my friend, and then my mother showed up to sit with me. She brought Elisha with her. I hadn't seen Elisha in several days, and I realized how much I had missed her! She was very shy, even to me. She wanted to make sure my hands were clean before I could even hug her. She was trying to deal with all the fears about Eli's illness, and we didn't have any answers for her. Scientist didn't even have answers. All I could do was hug her, kiss her, and try and reassure her that everything was going to be ok—somehow.

Finally, they told me Eli was done, and we began our journey back to the ICU. A dear friend sent me a text that said, "The greatest test of our character is our response to that which comes to make us quit." I have pondered that many times, and even though I felt I had moments of helplessness and hopelessness, one thing was for sure: I was not a quitter—and neither was my son! With God's help, we were going to endure this, and we were going to climb this mountain one inch at a time!

CHAPTER 5

HOPE UNVEILED

This hope we have as an anchor of the soul, both sure and steadfast, and which enters the Presence behind the veil.

-Hebrews 6:19 NKJV

On March 15, the doctors performed yet another spinal tap, and the same results came back. The medicine had all been administered, and now it was time to see God unveil His miracle working power. Even though I knew God had been working this whole time, I desired to see some of my hopes unveiled.

JOY FLOODS MY SOUL

It was evening time, and a new nurse had just come on duty. Eli had been responding well to the treatments given, but we wouldn't find out the extent of this syndrome until the doctors started weaning him off of the medicine that was helping him rest. The nurse was recording all his vitals, and I helped her change Eli's sheets and give him a bath. As I walked around the bed, I looked at my son's face, and I couldn't believe what I was seeing! His right eye lid was opening slightly, and I immediately asked the nurse about it. She turned to Eli and started asking him questions. "Eli, can you hear us? Eli, are you in pain?"

To all of these questions, he responded with the slightest turning of his head to say no. I couldn't believe it! Just that little nod made my heart jump, but God wasn't done yet.

The nurse then asked him, "Do you just want mom?"

With an up and down motion of his head, he nodded. My heart sank, and my whole being wanted to make this all better for him and just take him home. I was standing at his side, and I watched a tear roll down his little cheek. It broke my heart again. Oh, how I wished I could make this all better. I wished he didn't have to go through this. How many times had I asked God to let it be me instead of him? How could I watch him and not break down and cry? He needed me to be strong, but everything in me was broken and weak. When I looked at his face, I was a mess! I tried to hold back the tears, but they kept coming.

The pain I was feeling for my son changed when I reminded myself that yesterday he couldn't communicate at all but today the veil of hope was being lifted, and it turned my sadness to joy. I think it was at that moment that I knew that every step, no matter how big or small, would be a miracle from God. So at every stage, I would document what He had already done!

God started working overtime that day. Eli started breathing on his own and relying less on the ventilator. Even though he was still on the ventilator, he was responding by squeezing our hands and making hand gestures for us to figure out. Nothing on his body moved much, but at least it was moving, and he was starting to communicate with us.

STEADIED HOPE

As the days passed, Eli's body continued to improve. One of the things that I didn't realize until after we left the hospital was that, as Eli's nerves were starting to come back, it would be a very painful process. His body had attacked all his nerve endings, except those to his heart and his brain. Everything in his body had basically fallen asleep at the same time, and then as the nerves started to regenerate and fire again, he felt a tingling sensation. This process would continue for months, and in some parts of his body, it would continue for years. If someone touched his skin, he might think they were poking him with needles, yet in other places, he could feel nothing.

The next milestone was on March 17. Eli was learning to communicate about what he wanted and what he needed me to do. His fingers and his feet needed to be rubbed and stretched constantly. He also had a lot of itches where they had done the spinal tap. He could make signs with his hand that looked like a claw, and I would know that he had another itch. After one of our stretching sessions, which happened about every thirty minutes, I looked at him to ask him if he was okay. This time when I looked, I noticed that both eyelids had opened just a small amount, and I knew he wanted to look around. The muscles in his eyelids had been affected, but God was bringing strength back to them. I was so excited! I grabbed my bible, and I started praying Psalm 91 over him (NKJV).

He who dwells in the secret place of the Most High
Shall abide under the shadow of the Almighty.

I will say of the Lord, "He is my refuge and my fortress;
My God, in Him I will trust."
Surely He shall deliver you from the snare of the fowler
And from the perilous pestilence.
He shall cover you with His feathers,
And under His wings you shall take refuge;
His truth shall be your shield and buckler.
You shall not be afraid of the terror by night,
Nor of the arrow that flies by day,
Nor of the pestilence that walks in darkness,
Nor of the destruction that lays waste at noonday.
A thousand may fall at your side,
And ten thousand at your right hand;
But it shall not come near you.
Only with your eyes shall you look,
And see the reward of the wicked.
Because you have made the Lord, who is my refuge,
Even the Most High, your dwelling place,
No evil shall befall you,
Nor shall any plague come near your dwelling;
For He shall give His angels charge over you,
To keep you in all your ways.
In their hands they shall bear you up,
Lest you dash your foot against a stone.
You shall tread upon the lion and the cobra,
The young lion and the serpent you shall trample underfoot.
"Because he has set his love upon Me, therefore I will deliver him;

I will set him on high, because he has known My name.
He shall call upon Me, and I will answer him;
I will be with him in trouble;
I will deliver him and honor him.
With long life I will satisfy him,
And show him My salvation."

He watched me as I stood at the end of his bed and declared these scriptures over him. He watched as long as those little muscles could keep his eyes open, and then he drifted off to sleep.

The next morning, as the doctors did their morning rounds, they noticed that Eli had been breathing over the ventilator. This meant that they would consider taking it out as long as his lungs continued to improve. I felt an overwhelming sense of thankfulness. Thank you, God! Let it be today! I was ready to hear my baby's voice again. I was ready to hear his sweet laugh and kiss those cheeks, without tape and tubes all over them. After that amazing report, I got a phone call from my daughter—bless her heart. I had not had time to even think about her. I wondered how school was going and whether she was okay. My guilt session was interrupted by this sweet little voice, on the other end of the line, that was on the edge of crying. She held it together so she could tell me the dream she had that night. She said, "Mom, I had a dream, and I saw Eli walking into church." I was in tears on my side of the phone, knowing that God was giving hope to that little girl. She now had hope that her brother would be well one day, hope that we wouldn't have to be at the hospital forever, hope that we would all be together soon and everything would be all right.

A couple of hours passed, and I started noticing that Eli had a little more strength in his arms and legs. I asked him to try and pick them up, but all he could do was wiggle them a little. A little wiggle was all I needed to give God praise. Thank you, Lord, for renewed strength back into his legs, arms, eyes, and lungs!

The doctors soon entered with more amazing news. We were told that they were going to remove Eli from the ventilator, but he would have to wear a CPAP mask through the night until his oxygen levels went up. This was great news, but this news also brought some hesitation. I had never seen a CPAP mask before, but I was willing to try anything to hear his voice again. I stepped outside the room while they removed the ventilator, and when I went back, I grabbed his hand. I heard my little boy's voice whisper to me for the first time in six days. He said, "Mommy, I love you! Can we go home now?" My heart was leaping for joy from hearing his voice, but yet I was so sad that I could not pick him up and take him home right then. I felt such conflict of joy and pain: joy for the fact that he was alive and God was healing him but such pain that he had to go through all of this. I had both hope and disappointment. I had hope that Eli was going home someday, and yet disappointment that he wasn't healed before this disease took hold of his body. I'm not perfect, and I wanted God to tell me why this had to happen. However, I didn't have time to linger on my thoughts at that moment. All of my own questions would have to wait. I stood beside my son, and I could hear his voice again, and I wanted to hear everything he had to say.

That first night off the machine was very rough. The nurses brought the CPAP mask in, and it looked like something an air force pilot might need. I knew that it was not going to be easy for Eli to put on this mask. I recalled the last time they put a mask over his face: they were suffocating him to test his lung function. He had not forgotten that, and fear overtook him. He became scared of anyone who would enter his room. I kept telling him that he would need to wear this for just a few nights, until he could safely sleep through it. With his weak voice, he begged me not to make him wear it, not to put it over his face. Again, my heart was in such a peril. I knew he needed to wear it to stay off of the ventilator, but I heard the fear that was in my son's voice. I wanted to ease his pain. I wanted to make this all better for him. These were the moments when strength came to calm my son's fears and get the mask on him. It had to be one of the longest nights ever. After the mask was on, he would have panic attacks every thirty minutes. I would jump up and grab his hands and talk him back down every time. All of this was so physically and emotionally exhausting. By the morning, the nurse finally just took it off, and I was never more relieved.

After he took a short nap, the nurse said he could have an ice chip. He still had a feeding tube, but they wanted to see if he could eat the ice without choking. His face lit up with joy when he put that ice in his mouth. He said, "I had forgotten what water tasted like!"

During that day, they took out his catheter, and we all started praying that his bladder, and all the muscles surrounding those areas, had started working again. Otherwise, they would have to replace the catheter. Eli was praying so hard that they wouldn't have to do that. His IVs had started to leak, and now they were having to set a new line for the third time. It would have been different if his body was normal, but Eli's body was hypersensitive because of those nerves coming back. Even the simple act of taking his blood pressure brought tears and pain to him.

During all of these painful events, my husband and I started to pray with him. He suddenly began to pray on his own: "God, I will do anything you want me to do, but I need you right now, Jesus!" We knew his pain was great, but his fears were becoming greater. He feared that they would have to give him a shot, that they would have to squeeze his arm again, and that they would stick more tubes in him.

I couldn't blame him. I was tired of him being poked too, but he refused to take medicine for the pain. He didn't want to take a chance that the medicine might come in the form of a shot. I reassured him they would put it in his IV, but even that hurt badly, so he refused.

That next night, the doctors let him sleep without the mask, but he was being monitored closely. I knew how to monitor the numbers, so as I said goodnight to him and sat on the chair in the corner of the room. I watched. The numbers started out fine, but the deeper he slept, the lower the numbers went. I found myself dozing off, until I heard the alarm on his monitor. It was so loud and his numbers were too low. I jumped up and yelled, "Breathe, Eli! Breathe!" He woke up enough to take a few deep breaths, which raised his numbers, and the beeping stopped. This scenario happened all night. There is nothing like having to wake your child up just to make sure he will take another breath, that he will live another day, that he will just stay alive.

HOPE LIVES

My husband and I have traveled the world for medical missions, construction projects, and working at orphanages since 2011. There is nothing like going and serving those who have been cast out from their communities, and in some cases, their own countries. Each time we returned to America, we faced a difficult reality. It always seemed that most of our churches and most Christian homes had fallen asleep. The devil has lulled us into a place that is comfortable and cozy, and the only thought is for our immediate families and no more. Sometimes we are so selfish in our ambitions and dreams, and in the meantime, no one is standing in the gap for people who are really struggling. No one is praying for the men, women, and children who are really being persecuted for their faith in Jesus Christ. We pack the pews on Sunday but give no thought to anything outside of our little space.

Sometimes I think God is doing what I had to do in that hospital room that night. We keep falling into a deep sleep that could kill us, and something keeps yelling at us from deep within: "Breathe! It's time to awaken from that deadly sleep and breathe!" Breathe in His compassion, His love, His hopes, and His dreams, and He will make sure you have what you need. Matthew 6:33 says, **"But seek first the kingdom of God and His righteousness, and all these things shall be added to you"** (NKJV).

Let us wake up and be made whole! Let us pray that God will remove the veil that Satan has placed over our eyes. Help us, Lord, to delight and endure in these light afflictions, so that we may see your hand and feet at work here on this earth. Give us strength to live out our days selflessly.

ENDURING STILL

On March 21, Eli was able to drain his bladder without a catheter for the first time since he had been in the ICU. He started making some calls to family and friends and told them he was feeling much stronger. Day by day I had to keep reminding myself that he was getting better—and someday we would get to go home.

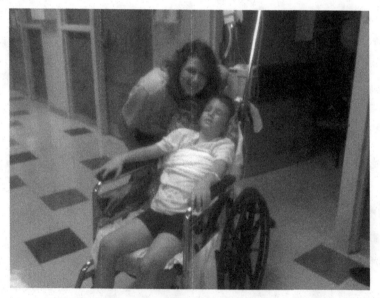

First time Eli was in a wheelchair

CHAPTER 6

HOPE RISES

But rise and stand on your feet; for I have appeared to you for this purpose, to make you a minister and a witness both of the things which you have seen and of the things which I will yet reveal to you.

—*Acts 26:16 (NKJV)*

It was March 23, and Eli continued to improve. Half of his face was still drooping, his eyelids would only open a small amount, and his eyes were not tracking together anymore. He still had not sat up or turned over by himself, but he was able to raise his arms a little higher every day.

The nurses came in that day and brought a wheelchair. I was thinking, *How in the world will we get him in there? He hasn't even sat up in eleven days! Please, God, help him!* They grabbed his little body and helped him rotate up to a seated position. He moaned loudly from the pain of being touched, but he quickly tried to gather himself. They let him try and sit without anyone touching him. He lasted for around five seconds, and then all the strength he had was gone. Five seconds sounds like a short amount of time, but for Eli it was amazing. I stood by his side and cheered him on the whole time.

Our next step was to get him in the wheelchair. Since he was unable to stand or hold himself, my husband and I took turns trying to lift him up and put him in the chair, without causing him any added pain. As we picked him up, we realized that his head just dropped back because of weak muscles in his neck. So, just as you would take care of a baby, we were now taking care of my precious nine-year-old boy, who couldn't do anything on his own once again.

The next day I got a phone call from my mother, who was keeping Elisha for a short time. I was told Elisha had not been feeling well, and she was now starting to run a fever. What was this? Had it not been enough with my son? My mom and I both feared it could be worse than a cold. I immediately got her an appointment with our doctor's office, which was not far from the hospital. My mom came to stay with Eli while I took my daughter. You could see the fear in her little face, and I knew I probably wasn't making it any easier on her because I didn't know what to expect. I tried to calm her nerves as the doctor came in the room. They went ahead and did blood work, just to make sure everything was okay. I started thanking God when we got the test results back and the diagnosis was bronchitis. Even though I was thinking that that was what they said about Eli too, I had a peace that she was going to be fine. The worst part for her was that she would not be allowed to visit Eli until she was better. As his body was trying to heal, he needed to stay away from anyone who might be sick.

Eli was really starting to miss his sister. She was so scared to see him lying in the bed with all those tubes that she wouldn't even get close to him. She also kept asking about his eyes, because she didn't like the way they looked. But he missed playing with her, talking to her, and just being a normal big brother. He enjoyed when people would come to see him. They would bring him gifts. His hands were so weak that he couldn't open most presents, but he would try so hard. I usually ended up opening the gift and helping him play with whatever they would bring. As soon as people would leave, he was back to sleep. He had little to no energy, and the doctors told us this would be normal for him for a long time. Even though the nerves in his face were not all working yet, he would still try and smile at everyone that would come and leave our room.

By March 27, we had officially been on this journey for twenty-two days. We had been moved out of the ICU and into a regular room. They were trying to get Eli to physical therapy once a day, but it was always a struggle. He enjoyed riding in the wheelchair, but after a short ride, he would be exhausted and want to lie down. He had lifted his head for the first time but was unable to eat food because of the continued paralysis of his facial muscles. So he still had a feeding tube and an IV for medicine. After consulting with doctors and physical therapists, we all concluded that the best option for Eli would be to transfer him to Scottish Rite Children's Hospital in Atlanta, Georgia. The hospital was well known for its rehabilitation of children who needed intense therapy. The transfer was approved.

YET ANOTHER BUMP IN THE ROAD

The night before we were to leave, I was approached by our nurse, asking me to sign a release that Eli could have another MRI before he left. I was very confused by this. We had not talked about this, and now at 10:00 p.m., they wanted to do another MRI. What? The nurse was being persistent, but I refused to sign anything. I was alone with my son, and at 12:00 a.m. that same night, the neurologist came into our room and wanted to discuss why I had not signed the release. I told him we had not discussed this with my husband, and I wasn't going to sign for any test without him knowing it. The doctor continued to try and tell me that Eli would need this, and he would have to be put back on a ventilator and return to the ICU for a few days more if we did this test. My stomach turned. I did not feel like this was in the best interest of my son, to go back through that. I refused to give in, and I kept pointing out that Eli had continued to get better every day. This whole conversation was happening right in front of Eli, and he was getting scared that something else was about to happen. So the doctor left, and it was resolved that we were going through no more testing. We were leaving for Atlanta as soon as possible.

On the morning of March 28 the ambulance arrived to take us to our new "home" for at least another four weeks. They strapped Eli onto a gurney and loaded us in the ambulance, and we left. This was Eli's first time riding in an ambulance, but he soon fell asleep and didn't remember the ride at all. As we arrived, they wheeled him into his new room. It was amazing—the bright colors, the peaceful smells. This didn't seem to be a hospital at all. I had such a peace about this place. It also had a large couch that folded out into a bed, a large window so that we could look outside, and plenty of room to maneuver his chair in and out of the room.

We were met by some very nice people, who helped us get comfy and gave us our schedule for the next day. We would have one day to rest, and then there would be therapy from 8:00 a.m. until 5:00 p.m. every day for the next four weeks.

Eli at the hospital in Atlanta

My alarm rang at 6:30 a.m. Wow! This was the first night Eli and I both got more than a couple hours of sleep. He rested so well, and I was up and ready to take a shower and begin a full day of therapy. The room had a large restroom and shower in it, so I was very thankful that I didn't have to leave the room. My ears were always attentive to listening for Eli's voice. When I finished getting ready, Eli was waiting for me, with his eyes wide open. He was very nervous about what the day would hold and was asking lots of questions that

I couldn't answer. I reassured him that this was going to be the place where they would push him hard, but he would be walking before we knew it. That said, anything more than one day felt too long! We were both very weary of the medicines, needles, and hospitals. If Jesus would just pass by right now and make him whole, we could go home and get on with our lives. But sometimes we have to climb the mountain in order to defeat it. I knew there were lessons to be learned with every step we took, so it was time for us to keep learning and climbing.

ONE STEP AT A TIME

I believe that we should never minimize the power of a step. As I look back on all the first steps I have taken, I see how God was there to meet me every time: when I took my first steps to trying out for a basketball team, to meeting my future husband, to walking down the aisle of an old wooden church and giving my heart to Jesus, to traveling on our first mission trip, or into and out of the hospital. Some were happy steps, and some were sad, but they were all steps that would mold us and change us forever.

The Bible says, "The steps of a good man are ordered by the Lord, and He delights in his way" (Psalm 37:23 NKJV). So does this mean that God delights in the man's way, or does the man delight in God's way, or does the man delight in his own way? I believe that God delights in man's ways when the man's steps are ordered by God. The reason I say this is that sometimes our steps are ordered by God and they are not delightful. Did Jesus think His steps were going to be delightful when he prayed that the cup might pass from Him while He was in the garden in Matthew 26:39? His steps brought pain upon himself but freedom for every man. His steps brought redemption. His steps brought grace. His steps brought life! So let us never underestimate the power of a step. When we take one step toward His will and His ways, He will take two steps toward us.

STEPPING INTO A NEW SEASON

Our first therapy day consisted of physical therapy, speech therapy, music therapy, and occupational therapy. Occupational therapy would be where they taught Eli how to do simple things, like eat with utensils, put on clothes, put on shoes, and brush his teeth. These seem like very easy tasks, but for someone who couldn't even sit up by himself, they were very hard things to accomplish. Our first morning, the OT sat his bed up and put a fork in his hand, and they practiced eating some food. He couldn't have real food yet, but at least they were working toward that day. She gave him a pen and asked him to write his name. He could barely hold the pen. It frustrated him that what once seemed so easy was now very hard to do. He managed to write his name in cursive on the paper, but even that small activity made him very tired. They also taught me how to better help him as he continued to get better.

Our next therapy was physical therapy. It was located in a large gym that they had down the hall. They came into the room and helped Eli get into a new pediatric wheelchair. This chair fit him a lot better and was very comfy for him to sit in. We pushed him down the hall, where they stood him up between two balance beams. The PT secured him from behind to see what he could and could not do.

I think sometimes we don't give ourselves enough credit—or should I say, we don't give the Holy Spirit within us enough credit. When push comes to shove, I believe He raises up within us and gives us the power to do what we could not do on our own. He gives us even more than we could hope, think, or imagine.

It was a great feeling to watch this amazing PT coach guide Eli in taking those first few steps. He had not been able to walk for sixteen days now. It was amazing to me how quickly something like walking could be taken from you and then how long it could take to get it back. He took his step, and with tears running down his face, he manned up and took seven more before he almost collapsed. What an awesome thing to watch! God gave us eight steps that day! Even though the pain was intense in his back and legs, Eli was so excited to be up on his feet again. That first day gave him hope that one day he would walk again.

We made it back to his room, where we put him back in the bed for a short rest before speech therapy. Eli's little body was exhausted, so he fell asleep as soon as he hit the pillow. They came to get him for his next therapy, and even though he didn't want to wake up, he did everything they asked. He enjoyed speech therapy. It was the easiest for him because the Guillain-Barré had not affected his mind. Even though he was slow at speaking and slurred his words, he knew exactly what all the tests were asking him to do. After watching him, they sent him down to do a swallow study. When he passed that test, the feeding tube could be removed. That feeding tube was a funny thing. Eli didn't realize that it went through his nose and into his stomach until my husband told him that one day. He was not happy with anyone touching it after that. Test results came back, and they were still not comfortable letting Eli swallow yet, but he could start sipping through a straw and eating some mashed up food.

By the end of the day, Eli's blood pressure was sky high. They knew that was probably a side effect from the treatment he was given for the Guillain-Barré. They were also getting false positives on things like Lyme disease and other illnesses. Those types of false positives were to be expected. Doctors decided to put him on a blood pressure medicine and a light pain reliever immediately.

Elisha visiting Eli in Atlanta

THE GRADUAL ASCEND

The days that followed were truly an uphill battle, but I was glad we were still in the fight. We counted his steps every day and thanked God daily that he was moving further along than the day before.

By April 18, Eli was discharged from the rehabilitation hospital and placed in a day rehab program. So we moved from sleeping in the hospital to sleeping in a hotel room, but we were very happy to be there. The hotels we stayed at had pools. After therapy every day, I would put him in his wheelchair and take him to the pool. I'll never forget the first time I put his little body into the water. He had always been a good swimmer, but the freedom the water gave him was so amazing. After a few minutes of swimming on his own, he looked up at me and said, "Mom, I love swimming! When I'm in the water, nobody can tell that I can't walk normal!" The pool became his therapy. It was a place to cope with everything that had happened. It was a place for us to hang out and let all the cares go, even if it was just for a little while. We often sang songs together as we swam. Those are the memories that I enjoy looking back on.

FRIENDS ALONG THE WAY

We had so many people who were praying for Eli and praying for our family that I would be afraid to mention one, in fear that I might leave someone out. But there was a dear family who lived in the Atlanta area while we were in the hospital there. They had a son named Myles, who was four years old at the time, and the mom would bring him to see Eli in the hospital, at our hotel room, and even at the swimming pool. Even though Eli was nine, he always looked forward to seeing Myles. Myles didn't look at Eli funny for the way he walked or talked or for how his eyes didn't track together all the time. He was just there being a crazy four-year-old boy, and he always brought a smile to Eli's face. It seemed the sillier Myles would get, the louder Eli would laugh, and that's exactly what Eli needed. After long hard days, Myles would storm into our hotel room, and the party began. Eli would sit and laugh and enjoy the company of someone who didn't look at his outward condition but would just play and be himself around him. That was truly a gift from God. Even when I think about him today, tears fill my eyes with the joy that Myles brought to Eli and myself during those rough days.

I believe that the devil's plans to hurt you will never be greater than the power of God to help you. God knew exactly what Eli needed. He knew exactly what I needed. Can we trust him? When it's dark, lonely, and with no end in sight, can we trust him? The answer is yes! Even when we cannot see Him or feel Him, we can always put our faith and hope in Him!

ANOTHER MOUNTAIN TO CLIMB

By May 7, Eli had single vision again. He was walking more without his wheelchair, and by May 25, we were released to go home for the first time. My husband decided to meet us in Atlanta and take us to the beach for a few days of relaxation before we went home. The picture that I saw in my mind when I looked at Eli in the PICU was of him on the beach playing. I took a picture the day we got him to the beach and let him sit and play in the sand. That will forever be a testimony to God's goodness and faithfulness.

Eli on the beach after leaving the hospital

Here are a few things that I have learned from all of this. First, what we worry about most is what we trust God with the least. I had to learn to trust that the God who had created Eli knew best how to take care of him. He knows the future and any plans. He knows Eli better than I could ever understand. God will help me as a mom to guide and direct, but His plans for Eli are greater than anything I could hope for or even imagine.

Someone wrote, "I'm not looking for the path of least resistance; I'm looking for the path where God gets the greatest glory." To say that's what I had dreamed of would be a lie. When it comes to our kids, we don't want any resistance. We want every day full of sunshine and roses. In the real world, the world that has fallen, that is just not reality, and anyone who claims to have it all together with a perfect life is just lying, or they simply have not lived long enough to have experienced the ups and downs of real life.

Eli and Elisha at the beach and back together again!

Elisha's dream did come true. When we returned home, Eli was welcomed back to church in grand style. As we drove onto the church parking lot, people stood holding signs and cheering for Eli. He got out of the car, and I was holding his walker in case he would need it. He turned to me and said, "Mom, I got this!" We walked all the way to the front of the church, where there was a seat for him. The cheering and applause was so loud that day. Elisha had seen it in the spirit before it was to come to pass, and on that day we celebrated. We celebrated God's love, His mercy, His unending faithfulness.

On August 7, Eli returned to school. Before this whole journey had begun, God had a plan that I would be introduced to one of the most amazing people I have ever met. From the moment we had our first parent-teacher meeting, I knew God was setting up Eli for the best school year ever. He was also setting me up to have a lifelong friend, who God would use in so many ways throughout that year. She would laugh with me and cry with me, and she always kept her eye on Eli, as if he was her own. To have this kind of person as a teacher meant everything to me. After taking care of him 24/7, it was now time to trust God again and let this wonderful teacher take care of him and teach him. She would call me and text me throughout the day, just to let me know how he was doing. I can't even begin to tell you the things God has done through this friendship, but I know it's just the beginning.

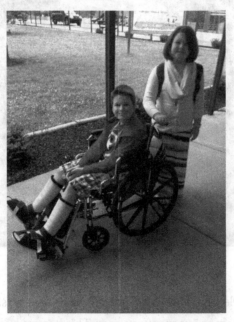

Returning to school after foot surgery

As I type this today, Eli is now a junior in high school. With help from an amazing guitar teacher God sent us, Eli continues playing guitar. Through all of his struggles, the devil could never take his love of music away from him. He continues to grow in his gifts. He is currently playing in youth services and with the main worship team on Sunday mornings at Canvas Community Church in Manchester, Tennessee. He also is involved with two young musicians' bands that meet every Friday in Brentwood, Tennessee.

Eli now enjoys playing his guitar.

The articles that I have read over the years have all said the effects of Guillain-Barré go away after a year. This has not been the case for

Eli. A year of recovering came with a surgery on both of his feet. He was unable to pull his feet up, so he developed what is known as "drop foot" on both feet. We are still believing God and working with a therapist using electrotherapy to aid in reviving those muscles. I still believe every morning when I wake up that this could be the day—this could be the day that Eli recovers all that was stolen from him over six years ago. My hope is in God when I can't stand on my own. My hope is in God when fears come against my praise. My hope is in God when I struggle to breathe. My hope is in God when the victories come.

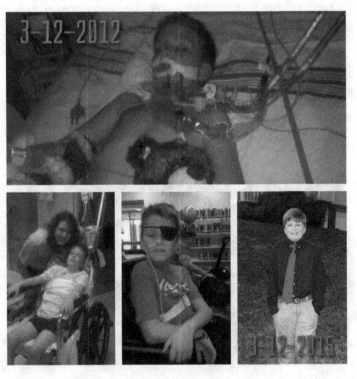

A few pictures of the journey

The Bible says, "But rise and stand on your feet; for I have appeared to you for this purpose, to make you a minister and a witness both of the things which you have seen and of the things which I will yet reveal to you" (Acts 26:16 NKJV). So today if you find yourself sitting down on God, it's time to rise and stand. It's time for you to see the victory through the smoke. It's time for you to walk in your purpose. It's time for you to be a witness of what God has done and is continuing to do in your life. This is a powerful scripture with a powerful message for everyone who has been "changed on the road!" Our hardships and difficulties serve to transform us into the image of Christ and also to give testimony to the grace and mercy of God.

God is faithful.
Eli, Elisha, and Nigel

THE SUMMIT

A long time ago there was a man named Jesus, who climbed a mountain of hope for us all. "He was wounded for our transgressions, He was bruised for our iniquities; the chastisement of our peace was upon him; and with his stripes we are healed" (Isaiah 53.5 NKJV). He hung there, died there, and rose again, so that one day we would be able to climb our mountains of hope.

We have all been wounded on the battlefield of life, but this one thing remains the same: God is for us and not against us. He will give us the equipment we need to climb the next mountain. We cannot and will not accept defeat or compromise. No devil can take that love away from us, which God has given us, through His son Jesus Christ! So we must keep climbing. We must keep going because the summit is just ahead!

ABOUT THE AUTHOR

Gina Davis is a wife and a stay at home mom of two amazing children. She and her husband Richie have been married for 25 years. They ran a very successful dental practice and founded a non-profit organization, Beyond Religion Ministries. They have traveled to over 12 different nations working in remote medical clinics, construction projects and loving on orphans all over the world.

Printed in the United States
By Bookmasters